MAR 1 8 2004

A Day With
HOMO HABILIS

LIFE 2,000,000
YEARS AGO

APR 1 7 2004

DR. FIORENZO FACCHINI

A Day With
HOMO HABILIS

LIFE 2,000,000
YEARS AGO

Illustrations by
ALESSANDRO BALDANZI

TWENTY-FIRST CENTURY BOOKS / BROOKFIELD, CONNECTICUT

English translation copyright © 2003 by Twenty-First Century Books
Originally published by Editoriale Jaca Book spa
Via Gioberti 7,
20123, Milano, Italy
www.jacabook.it

Library of Congress Cataloging-in-Publication Data
Facchini, Fiorenzo, 1929-
[Fiorenzo Facchini racconta la giornata di un Homo habilis. English]
A day with Homo habilis : life 2,000,000 years ago / Fiorenzo Facchini;
illustrations by Alessandro Baldanzi.
p. cm.   (Early humans)
Translation of: Fiorenzo Facchini racconta la giornata di un Homo habilis.
Includes index.
Summary: Describes an imaginary day of a family of homo habilis, the earliest species of humans.
ISBN 0-7613-2765-7 (lib. bdg.)
1. Homo habilis—Juvenile literature. 2. Paleolithic period, Lower—Africa, Eastern—Juvenile literature.
3. Prehistoric peoples—Africa, Eastern—Juvenile literature. 4. Africa, Eastern—Antiquities—Juvenile literature.
[1. Prehistoric peoples. 2. Fossil hominids.] I. Baldanzi, Alessandro, ill. II. Title. III. Series.

GN770.42.E37 F3313 2003
960'.1—dc21   2002014541

Published by Twenty-First Century Books
A Division of The Millbrook Press, Inc.
2 Old New Milford Road
Brookfield, Connecticut 06804
www.millbrookpress.com

Printed in Italy
2 4 5 3 1

CONTENTS

FOREWORD

Beside some of the illustrations and text in this book, you will see arrows pointing toward pictures of prehistoric art, which are far, in time and space, from the life of *Homo habilis*. Some themes already beginning to develop in the life of *Homo habilis* have been important in all human artistic expression. The pictures beside the arrows will show how culture has had a greater and greater influence on human behavior since the time of *Homo habilis*. Even if it is not easy to pinpoint cultural elements at the dawn of human existence (given the scarce amount of documented evidence), one must conclude that there was a certain amount of cultural influence on the evolution of humankind. The links between physical and cultural evolution are not yet clear, but one must not forget that all the evidence the researcher has available is in the form of fossils: primarily, the tools made and used by humans.

It is through tools we understand that the first humans belonging to the genus *Homo* produced culture—that is, a deliberate way of interacting with the environment and expressing information learned and transmitted through space and time. In their encounters with the environment, the first humans manifested not only cerebral evolution but also a capacity for reflection and planning.

Graphic and artistic representations are ways in which humans communicate and are a basic means by which humankind has characterized itself all over the world at all times in human history. That which is most evident in the testimony of recent prehistoric epochs can also be gathered in some of the much earlier phases of human experience.

INTRODUCTION

ENTERING THE WORLD
OF *HOMO HABILIS*

INTRODUCTION

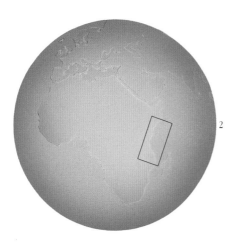

2. The highlighted area on the globe shows the region in Africa where the most important discoveries about humanity's origins were made.

1. This drawing shows how Olduvai Gorge in Tanzania might have looked at the time of Homo habilis.

Two to three million years ago, the Earth looked very different from how it looks today.

Today's Europe, Asia, and North America were mostly forests and woods. In Africa, to the east of the Great Rift Valley, where large lakes are situated now, vast areas of savanna and grasslands made suitable terrain for two-legged locomotion, or bipedalism. The Australopithecines, who lived in this part of Africa, were the non-human primates who practiced bipedalism, although not as we do today.

Another more evolved being, very similar to us although smaller in size, also lived in this open environment: *Homo habilis*. The male stood about 59 inches (150 centimeters) tall. His brain capacity was smaller than ours, but larger than that of *Australopithecus* (by about 40 percent). His cranial capacity varied from about 43 to

3. This is a depiction of the environment in which Homo habilis *and* Australopithecus *both lived.*

4. Here is a comparison of the brains of Australopithecus *and* Homo habilis: *The brain of* Homo habilis *is larger and more complex.*

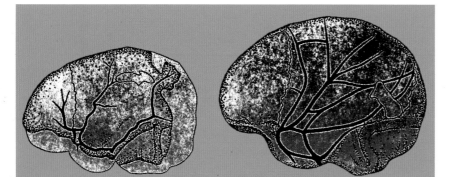

49 cubic inches (700 to 800 cubic centimeters). The imprints of nerve areas that relate to articulate speech have been found on the internal walls of the skull: the Broca's Area for the emission of sounds, and the Wernicke's Area for the comprehension of sounds.

5. This is the landscape near Hadar, in the Afar region of Ethiopia. Although the area is well known for discoveries about Australopithecus, *this panorama is a good example of a region with open spaces, suitable to bipedalism and the life of the first humans.*

6. This drawing shows the anatomical muscle structures needed for bipedalism.

7. A comparison between the skeletal structures of a man and a gorilla. The two pictures show the man's completely erect posture, with his head balanced at the top of his spinal cord and the pelvis positioned to shift the body's weight to the hind limbs. If these two conditions are not present, the body cannot stand erect and becomes stooped.

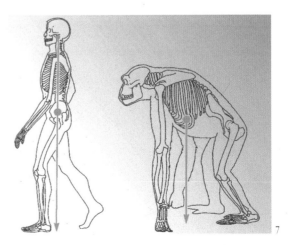

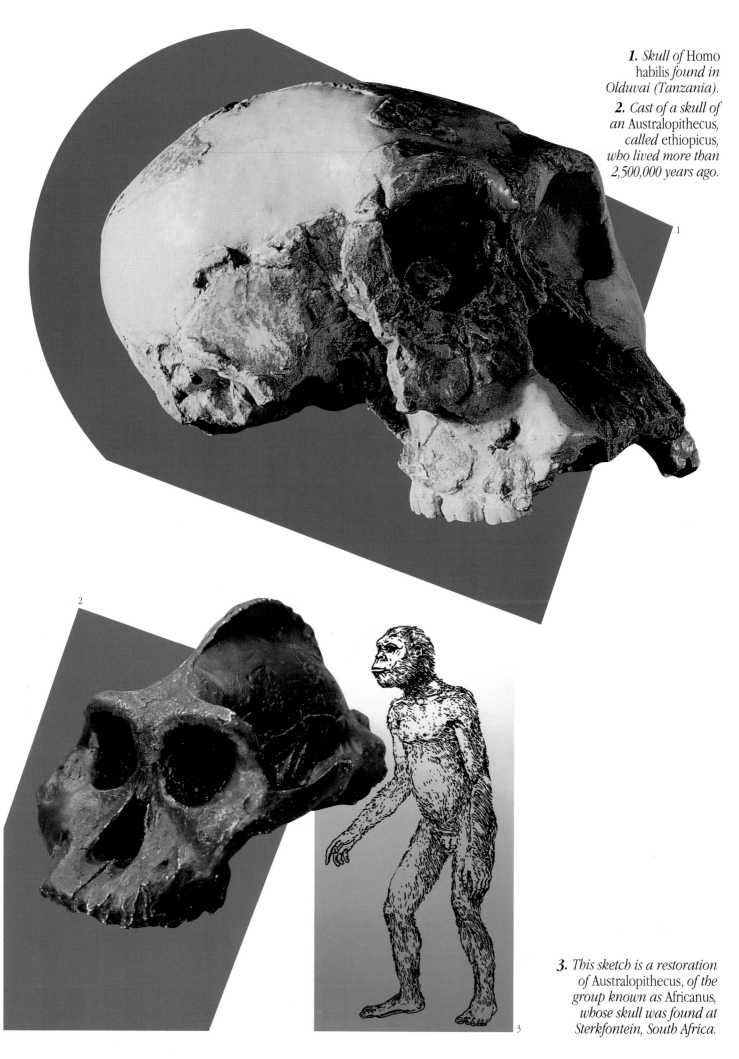

1. *Skull of* Homo habilis *found in Olduvai (Tanzania).*
2. *Cast of a skull of an* Australopithecus, *called* ethiopicus, *who lived more than 2,500,000 years ago.*

3. *This sketch is a restoration of* Australopithecus, *of the group known as* Africanus, *whose skull was found at Sterkfontein, South Africa.*

The face of *Homo habilis* was less prominent than that of the *Australopithecus*. The teeth were adapted to an omnivorous diet, just like the teeth of modern-day humans. *Homo habilis* flaked flint and made tools with sharp cutting edges on one or both faces. They made tools systematically and took good care of them because they were essential for obtaining food. We can make this conclusion because tools are frequently found associated with skeletal remains. The tool-making skills of the Hominid of that epoch has earned the designation *Homo "habilis,"* which means "handy man."

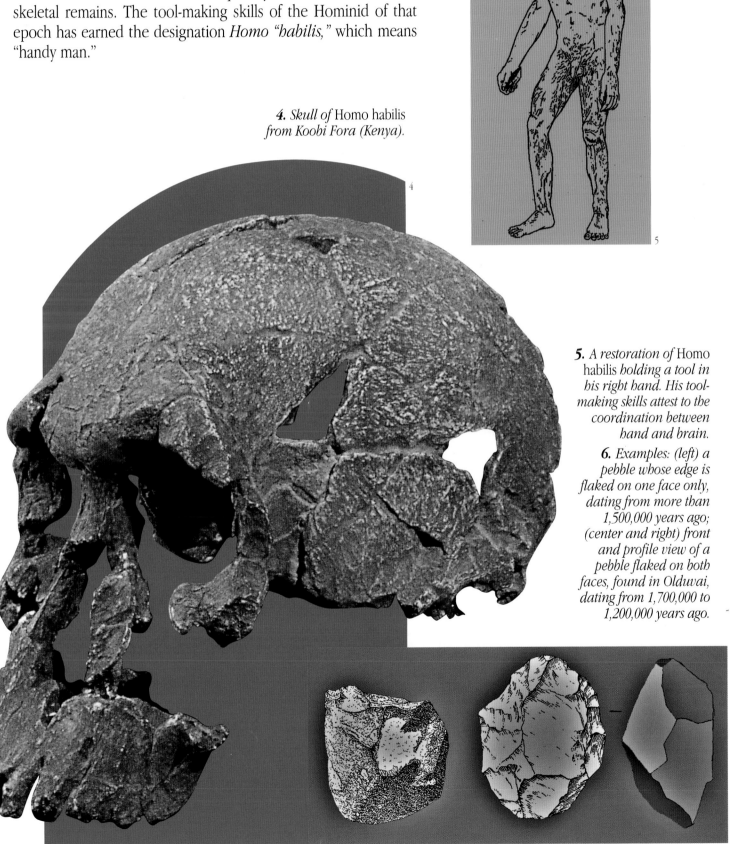

4. *Skull of* Homo habilis *from Koobi Fora (Kenya).*

5. *A restoration of* Homo habilis *holding a tool in his right hand. His tool-making skills attest to the coordination between hand and brain.*

6. *Examples: (left) a pebble whose edge is flaked on one face only, dating from more than 1,500,000 years ago; (center and right) front and profile view of a pebble flaked on both faces, found in Olduvai, dating from 1,700,000 to 1,200,000 years ago.*

Homo habilis used the instruments to hunt small animals, to skin them, and to cut the meat from them. Being omnivorous, he ate berries, fruits, and other vegetables.

The best places to live were close to lakes or bodies of water. *Homo habilis* set up camps. Traces of these have been found in the form of circles of stones that served as the bases of huts. Remains of animals, presumably eaten by *Homo habilis*, and tools made of stone were found inside these circles. The small prey (which could also have been bodies of zebras killed by large cats) were not eaten immediately. They were brought back to the camps to be divided among the other members of the family, mostly women and children who had stayed at home.

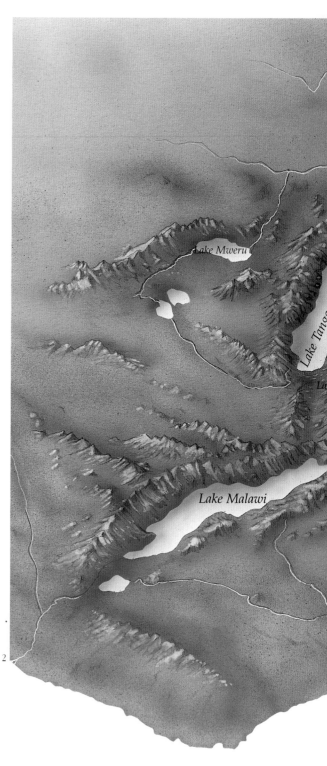

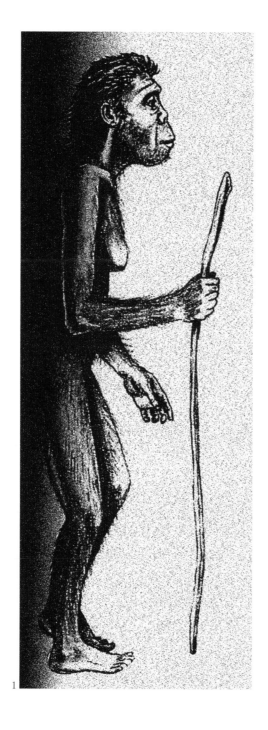

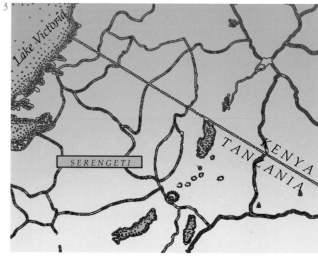

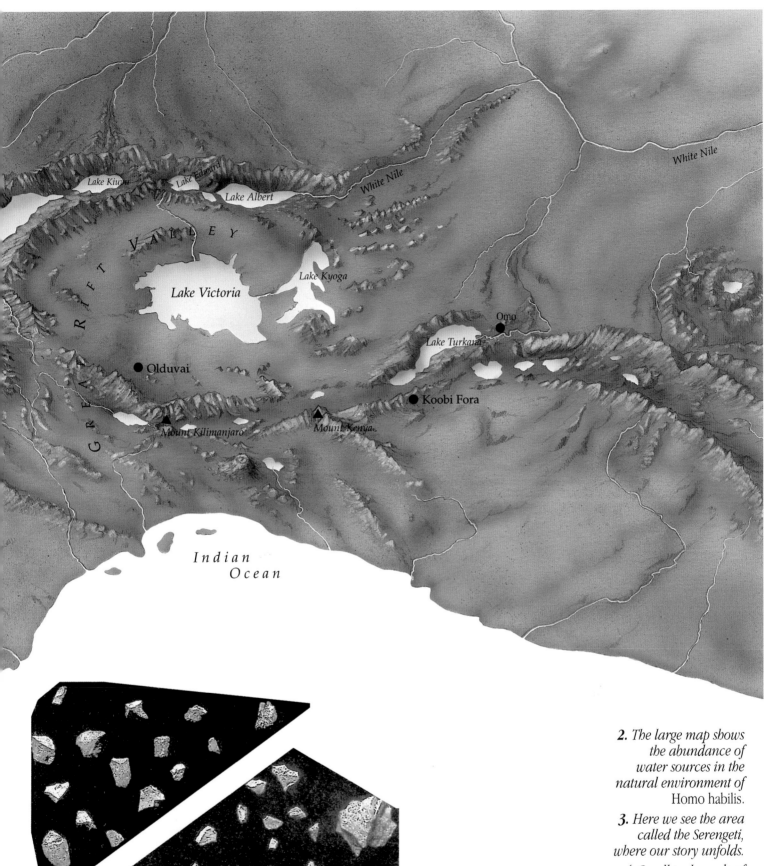

2. The large map shows the abundance of water sources in the natural environment of Homo habilis.

3. Here we see the area called the Serengeti, where our story unfolds.

4. Small tools made of stone that were found at Koobi Fora (Kenya), dating from about 1,800,000 to 1,600,000 years ago.

1. *A woman seems to be scanning the horizon. In her hand she holds a cane that the first humans used and made themselves. Homo habilis was able to organize living space, and also knew how to explore wider territories. Since it is thought that an increase in brain size can mean a longer dependence on one's parents, the role of the woman in the family setup becomes crucial.*

In places that *Homo habilis* frequented, special areas have been identified for cutting stones and bones, and other areas for butchering animals.

One may ask if *Homo habilis* knew how to speak. We have no fossils to tell us about language. But *Homo habilis* probably made simple sounds that had meaning. The species had the neurology for articulate speech. What we know of the activities of *Homo habilis* shows that they probably transmitted culture through language. Remains attributed to *Homo habilis* have been found in various parts of eastern Africa: in the valley of the Omo River (Ethiopia), in Koobi Fora to the east of Lake Turkana (Kenya), in the Olduvai Gorge (Tanzania); in southern Africa: in Malawi, and in Sterkfontein (South Africa). The remains found near Lake Turkana show more cerebralization (up to 49 cubic inches, or 800 cubic centimeters) and have been attributed to a species called *Homo rudolfensis*.

Homo habilis lived 2.5 million to 2 million years ago. In *Homo habilis* we find the oldest expression of humankind.

It is believed that *Homo erectus* was the descendant of *Homo habilis*.

4

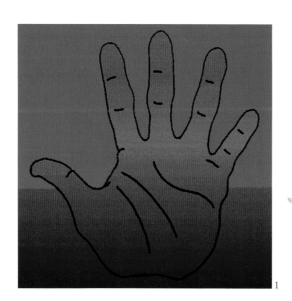

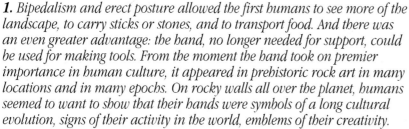

2

3

1. Bipedalism and erect posture allowed the first humans to see more of the landscape, to carry sticks or stones, and to transport food. And there was an even greater advantage: the hand, no longer needed for support, could be used for making tools. From the moment the hand took on premier importance in human culture, it appeared in prehistoric rock art in many locations and in many epochs. On rocky walls all over the planet, humans seemed to want to show that their hands were symbols of a long cultural evolution, signs of their activity in the world, emblems of their creativity.

2. The arrow points toward an example of the theme of hand imprints that show up in a rock painting in Tanzania from recent prehistory.

3. Hands painted on a rock in South Africa (about first to fourth century C.E.).

4. Let us imagine Homo habilis *not only capable of designing tools, organizing encampments, and finding food, but also capable of observing nature, its resources, its subtle signs. The river pebbles in the picture might have been used by* Homo habilis *in some way.*

● Omo

Koobi Fora ●

Olduvai ●

Sterkfontein ●

5. *Rocky walls in Tanzania that may have offered shelter to* Homo habilis.

6. *Landscape of Malawi, a place where much evidence of* Homo habilis *has been found.*

7. *On the small map: some of the most well-known sites where fossils of* Homo habilis *have been found.*

The chart at right shows the succession of the evolutionary line, or phylum, from the large class of Mammals to the order of Primates and then to Humans. From the order of Primates, we note the Superfamily of Hominoids—large monkeys such as baboons and their descendants—and from this Superfamily, in turn, we are interested in the family of Hominids, which includes the genus Australopithecus *and* the genus Homo. *The genus Homo does not produce various species, but rather one species in various forms. And so, from the systematic point of view used in natural science, every human is a Mammal, Primate, Hominoid, Hominid, Homo.*

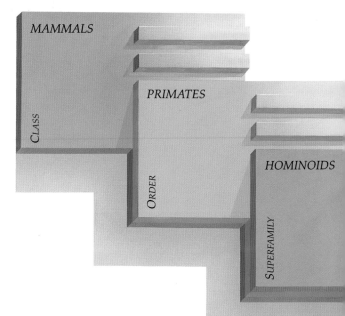

MAMMALS

PRIMATES

HOMINOIDS

CLASS

ORDER

SUPERFAMILY

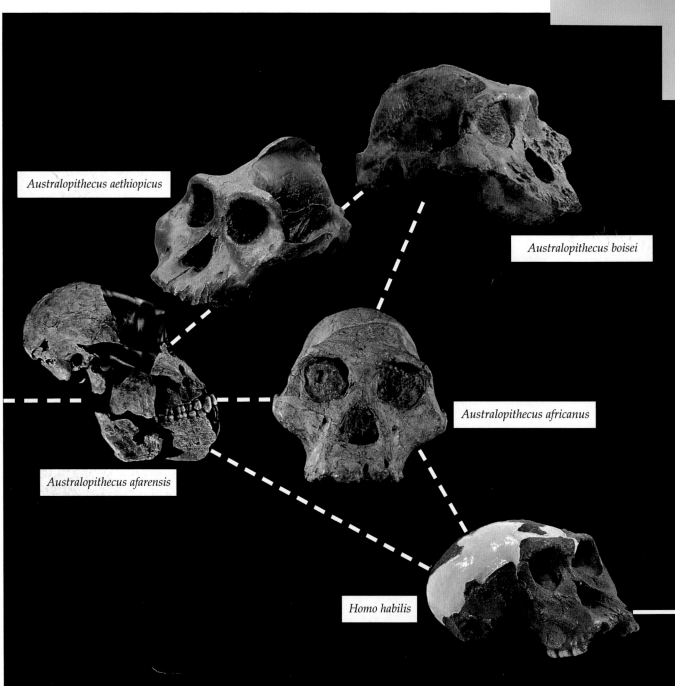

Australopithecus aethiopicus

Australopithecus boisei

Australopithecus africanus

Australopithecus afarensis

Homo habilis

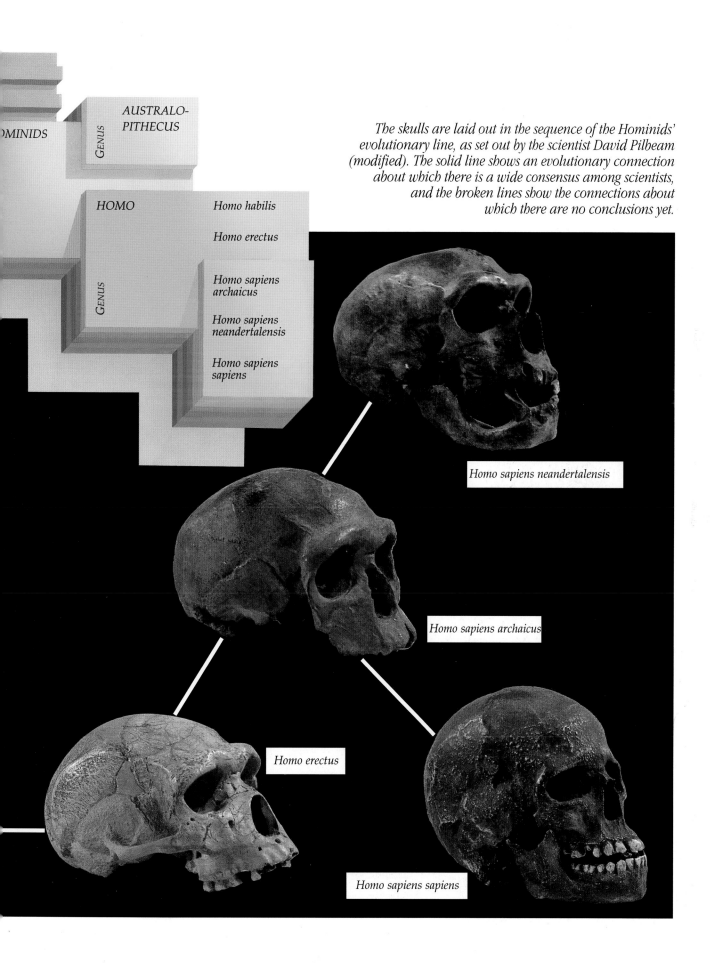

AUSTRALO-PITHECUS

GENUS

OMINIDS

HOMO

GENUS

Homo habilis

Homo erectus

Homo sapiens
archaicus

Homo sapiens
neandertalensis

Homo sapiens
sapiens

*The skulls are laid out in the sequence of the Hominids'
evolutionary line, as set out by the scientist David Pilbeam
(modified). The solid line shows an evolutionary connection
about which there is a wide consensus among scientists,
and the broken lines show the connections about
which there are no conclusions yet.*

Homo sapiens neandertalensis

Homo sapiens archaicus

Homo erectus

Homo sapiens sapiens

WATU'S DAY

WATU AND HIS FAMILY

A few families, made up of adults (parents, uncles, and aunts) and children, have set up a small camp on the banks of a river. Among them are Watu, his wife, and their three children. Watu is the oldest in the group and is respected by the men of the other families for his authority.

A short time ago, they settled here, traveling back from the Serengeti Plain in Tanzania along the river to keep themselves safe from the savanna's predators, the dangerous large cats such as the leopard and the lion. They still remember when one of the group went off alone, away from the camp. He never returned. He was found torn to pieces by a leopard and picked clean by a hyena.

The camp is on a plateau of the African Rift, more than 6,562 feet (2,000 meters) high. Some of this region is forest, some is savanna with a few sparse trees. Various rocky out-croppings stick up here and there. They are very valuable because of the basic raw material that they supply for making tools. Living together, the families can help one another find food and defend themselves against fierce animals.

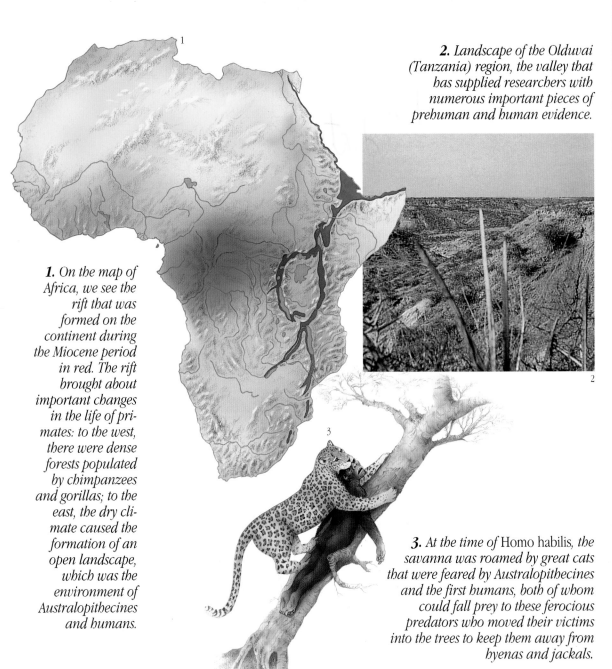

2. Landscape of the Olduvai (Tanzania) region, the valley that has supplied researchers with numerous important pieces of prehuman and human evidence.

1. On the map of Africa, we see the rift that was formed on the continent during the Miocene period in red. The rift brought about important changes in the life of primates: to the west, there were dense forests populated by chimpanzees and gorillas; to the east, the dry climate caused the formation of an open landscape, which was the environment of Australopithecines and humans.

3. At the time of Homo habilis, *the savanna was roamed by great cats that were feared by Australopithecines and the first humans, both of whom could fall prey to these ferocious predators who moved their victims into the trees to keep them away from hyenas and jackals.*

THE DWELLING

We enter Watu's hut and find his wife and three children. The hut, like that of other families, is built on a stone base and made of interwoven branches that come together at the top to form a dome.

Inside, the family finds shelter from the sun's burning rays during the day and protection from animals during the night.

The hut is circular, about 13 feet (4 meters) in diameter. Humans naturally chose the circular shape for its efficiency and economy. This shape matches that of the sun and the moon.

The little ones in the family stay inside the hut during the day. At night, Watu divides up the food. The space near the hut is where the little ones play.

The camp is set up near flowing water. Being near water is essential to life. A body of water is also a good place for hunting animals (such as antelopes, gazelles, and gnus), which can be caught easily when they come there to drink.

1. The river near Melka-Kunturé (Ethiopia), where remains of Homo habilis *have been found.*
2. At Olduvai (Tanzania), a discovery was made of a circular area of about 172 square feet (16 square meters), bordered by stones, thought to be the wall of a hut dating from 1,800,000 years ago. In the drawing, the tools are orange, the bones are yellow, the stone circle is gray.

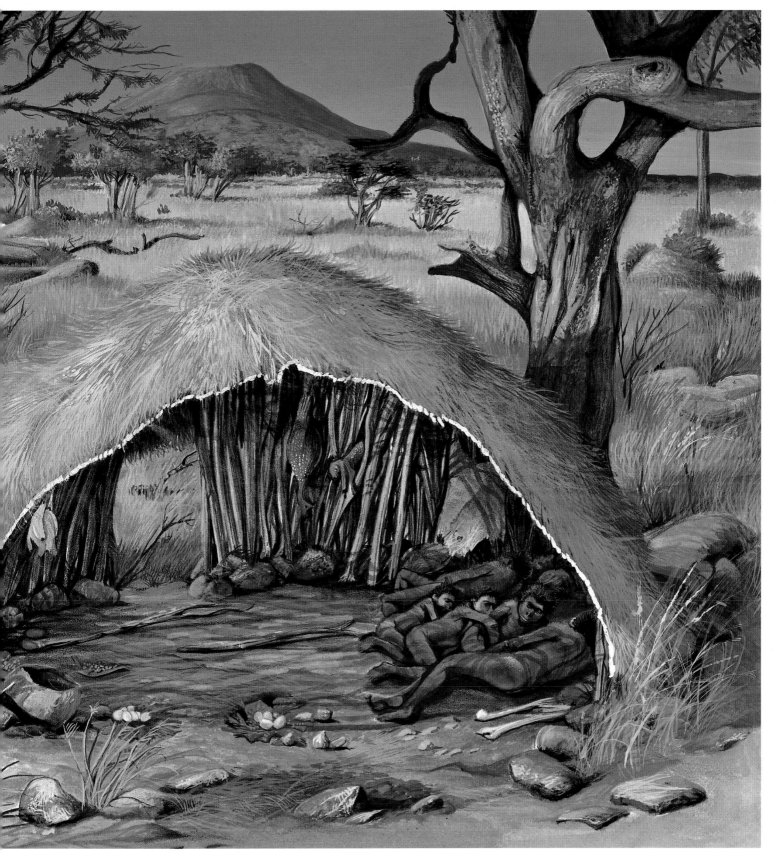

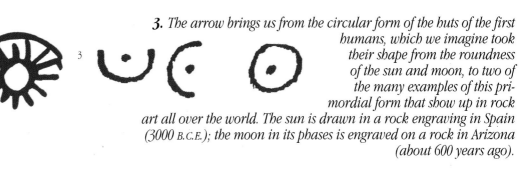

3. *The arrow brings us from the circular form of the huts of the first humans, which we imagine took their shape from the roundness of the sun and moon, to two of the many examples of this primordial form that show up in rock art all over the world. The sun is drawn in a rock engraving in Spain (3000 B.C.E.); the moon in its phases is engraved on a rock in Arizona (about 600 years ago).*

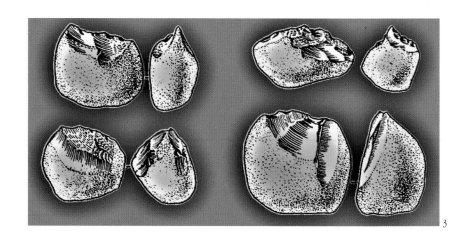

1. *A large chopper discovered in the oldest stratum at Melka-Kunturé, Ethiopia (1,700,000 – 1,600,000 years ago). Like others from this site, it is a river pebble transformed into a tool by having been flaked on one face.*

2. *Two stones, one for striking (the "hammer") and one (the "nucleus" or "core") to be transformed into a tool with a sharp edge by detachment of one or more parts ("flakes"). This was the first human toolmaking activity. Humans had a well-developed thumb that was completely opposable to the other fingers, which allowed them the strength necessary for gripping stones in this phase of their work.*

3. *This drawing shows four pebble tools (front and profile view) that were gathered at Olduvai (Tanzania).*

THE DAY BEGINS

The rhythm of the day is linked to the daylight hours. It is early morning (perhaps 5 A.M.). The sun is already high on the horizon. The clear sky is an intense blue. Multicolored birds fly high in the sky.

While the children are still asleep, the women go down to the river to get water that they carry in large gourds. Along the way they gather pods and fruit.

Watu and the other men have gone off to explore the land in search of food, bringing stones and sticks with them. But not all the men have left the camp. Some of them have stayed behind to help the women and children and to work cores of flint they brought home last night. It is also useful to have some men nearby in case unwanted guests visit.

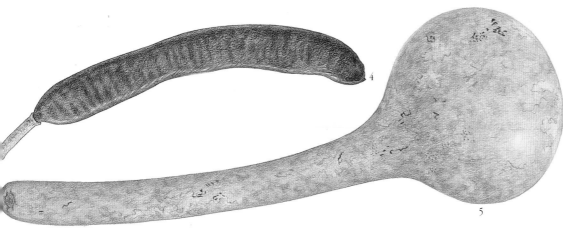

4. A dried pod. Legumes, with nutritious seeds enclosed by two membranes, were an important part of the diet of early humans.

5. A gourd, probably the oldest container used by humankind. Because gourds come in various sizes and dimensions and do not spoil, they can be cut, dried, and used as receptacles.

IN SEARCH OF FOOD

The small band of men from the savanna, guided by Watu and armed with sticks and stones, go into the tall grass on a plateau dotted with baobab and acacia trees.

As the men come closer, baboons observe them with curiosity. Walking along the river, the men do not go too far from the camp. At a certain point, an unusual sight catches their attention: a lioness crouching over a zebra that has been torn to bits. The zebra was her prey. Not too far off, a hyena waits his turn. But as soon as the sated lioness leaves, our men throw themselves onto the zebra's bleeding body and use their sticks and stones to chase away the hyena who tries to come close.

At a certain point, a cloud of dust rises. Watu warns the group that elephants are coming. They should not be too worried. All they need to do is hide. Elephants love to eat fruit. It's best to stay far away from their trunks, which they use to grasp things and throw them up into the air.

Once the elephants have passed, Watu and the other men use choppers to cut up the zebra. They hang the body parts on their sticks and bring them back to the camp.

1

1. Scene of the Omo (Ethiopia) region, which has been essential in the study of Hominids and in reconstructing the environments that characterized human evolution there.

2. The Dinotherium, indigenous to Africa, at the time of the first humans.

3. The picture beside the arrow shows us the future that large animals were to have in human prehistoric art. Humans felt that they were a part of nature and that animals were a part of their lives. Artistic expression shows up everywhere and in all time periods. Since large animals were impressive to the human mind, humans replicated them in art, not only because of their magnificence but also because they seemed larger than life. Here we see a rock engraving from Egypt (about 10,000 B.C.E.) of elephants and giraffes. A few human beings appear to be looking on.

1. *Area of a camp (Melka-Kunturé, Ethiopia) where evidence of human activity was found. It appears that special areas were set apart for making tools. In the photo: pebble tools and remains of animals.*

HUNTING FOR SMALL ANIMALS

People of the savanna are clever. They eat things that grow in their environment: fruit, roots, berries, and small and medium-size animals. Sometimes they use traps to catch birds and small mammals such as hares and young antelopes. Hunting for birds like ptarmigans, guinea fowls, and roosters is easier. It is easy to carry them back to the camp. Their meat is delicious and tender, not tough like zebra or antelope meat. As Watu is bringing the quartered zebra home, he detects a movement in the tall grass. Perhaps it is a bird that has become entangled in it. The men approach and easily capture a guinea fowl.

In the early afternoon the hunters are back home. They find some men busy working flint. Others have gone out around the area of the camp in search of more food for themselves and for the women and children who stayed behind in the camp.

4. *The chart illustrates the expansion over time of two orders of small mammals that may have been* hunted by Homo habilis: *rodents and lagomorphs.*

2. *A ptarmigan. Still in existence today and similar to the pheasant, the ptarmigan likes to walk on the ground between flights. This made them easy for* Homo habilis *to catch.*

3. *A rare fossilized feather, about 50,000,000 years old. Evidence shows that birds existed long before humans did.*

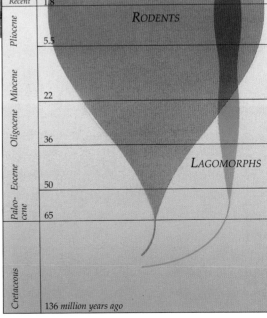

Recent	1.8	RODENTS
Pliocene	5.5	
Miocene	22	
Oligocene	36	
Eocene	50	LAGOMORPHS
Paleo-cene	65	
Cretaceous	136 *million years ago*	

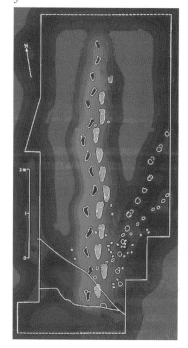

AUSTRALOPITHECINE FRIENDS

On an afternoon excursion, a small group of men from the savanna goes out to the edge of the forest. Suddenly, they are surprised to see other beings who look a lot like them; they walk the same way, but they have much longer arms and somewhat smaller heads. Watu has come across them before and assures the others that they are not dangerous. They are more like humans than like monkeys, he says. They are the Australopithecines.

They move a little clumsily, swinging along on their legs, but they are very adept at climbing trees. They are being chased by two hyenas. Some have climbed up trees; others find safety by running away. And here comes our team of men, who, armed with sticks, attack the hyenas and chase them away.

The Australopithecines, amazed, watch them, then run and hide in the forest. They understand now that these men are not enemies.

1. *Landscape of the Tanzanian savanna, where* Homo habilis *and* Australopithecus *both lived at the same time.*

2. *Forest to the west of the Rift Valley. The wooded area must have been more familiar to the ancestors of the Australopithecines, who were not yet completely adapted to an open environment.*

3. *A series of footprints discovered at Laetoli (Tanzania), imprinted in the volcanic ash, 3,600,000 years ago. In red, we see smaller footprints; in the center, in yellow, larger footprints; both are from earlier forms of* Australopithecus *and show that this being was able to walk erect. Over time, their descendants improved their bipedalism and were able to live outside the forest.*

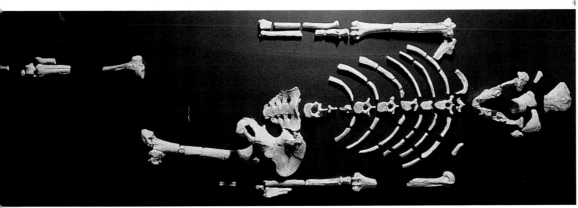

4

4. *Not far from Addis Ababa (Ethiopia), in the Afar region, a female skeleton of the archaic* Australopithecus *was found. The skeleton reveals that this being already had acquired the ability to walk on two legs; it must have been an ancestor of the form of* Australopithecus *that* Homo habilis *would have known.*

LIFE IN THE CAMP

Back from hunting, Watu and the other men rest near the huts and work stones.

    The women are with the children. A young woman is nursing a baby in front of a hut. Another woman is holding a child by the hand and teaching him to walk. Yet another is pointing out things to go and fetch, such as small stones, branches, or flowers. They use words to make themselves understood, or small noises with hand gestures.

    Some of the women and children leave the camp to explore the area and see what they can find to eat. Watu instructs them: "Gather and eat what you find. Watch out for snakes that may be hiding in the plants. Sticks will be useful for this."

    One boy climbs an acacia tree and picks pods. A child catches a large grasshopper. Another child, who is luckier, finds a nest with bird's eggs in a tree. This is tasty food for children.

    They gather berries from bushes. They break open the ends of the perennial grasses to gather seeds. They eat some of them and fold up the rest in large leaves to bring home. The most desirable fruits are the mango and banana. They eat some of them with great pleasure, but also bring some back to the hut.

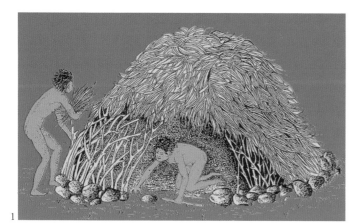

2. Near the arrow: three statuettes of women. The first, from Austria, dates from 32,000 years ago, when in Central Europe there was a sudden appearance of carved human figures and symbolic objects, perhaps related to fertility.

3. From Sardinia, 5000 B.C., a mother and child, symbolic of the protection of life.

4. In terracotta, this could be the representation of a divinity, found in a tomb in Moldavia (about 3500 B.C.).

1. The drawing shows a hut with a man and woman at work. In the camp, the woman's role was extensive childcare, providing food (particularly by gathering wild fruits), and intense involvement with domestic life. Womanhood, then, evokes the rhythms of fertility and birth and gives rise, in the future, to reflection and artistic expression.

3. *Millipedes, cockroaches, grasshoppers. Based on when they lived, they may have been part of the diet of* Homo habilis.

1. *A fossilized African mole cricket dating from several million years ago.* Homo habilis *may have been familiar with this type of insect.*

2. *An insect that has been fossilized in Baltic amber, a tree resin that surrounds and captures insects that are on the trunk, preserving them for tens of thousands of years. Which suggests that* Homo habilis, *even in another environment, may have looked for insects on trees.*

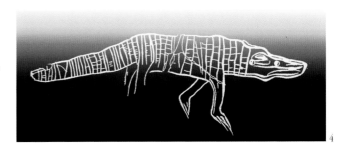

4. Long, long ago, when the Sahara was green and teeming with life, a prehistoric artist carved a crocodile in a rocky wall in the Libyan desert. The reptile takes up a good 8 feet (2.5 meters) of rock. This graphic expression of the crocodile's ferocity comes out of a time not so different from our own. Homo habilis *tried to understand and make others understand the dangers hidden in and around bodies of water.*

ON THE BANKS OF THE RIVER

On the banks of the river, Watu's son Wubu is having fun using a stick and stone to dig for insects. After a while he looks up to see something strange coming out of the water. His father told him to watch out for crocodiles that can suddenly appear.

The next moment, he notices a guinea fowl not far off. He makes a motion to his older brother, who is near the hut, to come and catch it. Together, they push it into the water, as they have seen the grown men do. This is how they capture it.

At home, they are praised for the skills they have shown. Watu offers a prize for his sons' achievement: a fruit for each of them.

WORKING FLINT

In the afternoon, the group that returned with the zebra spreads out around the hut to cut the zebra into pieces and distribute it for food. Watu always takes charge of this work, using a large, sharp flake of stone. But it is not dinnertime yet. The others have to come back from their short excursions.

Other men are busy making tools. They use a hard stone hammer to detach flakes from stream cobbles. The flakes have sharp points and edges that will be useful not only for cutting meat but also for cutting up the skins of animals.

The men teach some of the boys how to make tools (choppers and chopping tools) from pebbles. Some of the flakes are large and heavy; they will be good for breaking the bones of animals and for extracting the marrow, which is a delicious food. Other small and more finely worked flakes will be brought on the hunt and used for butchering animals that they kill or find already dead.

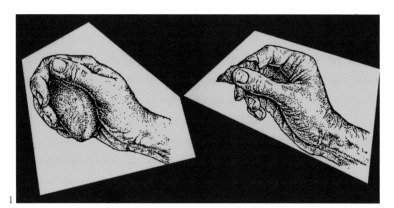

1

1. The thumb of Homo habilis *was well-developed and opposable to the other fingers. The ball of the thumb on the ball of the opposing finger allows for a strong grip (left) and also for handling small objects with a precise grip (right).*

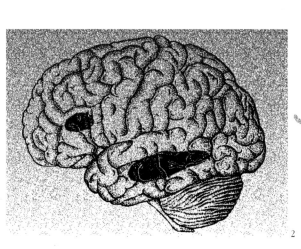

2

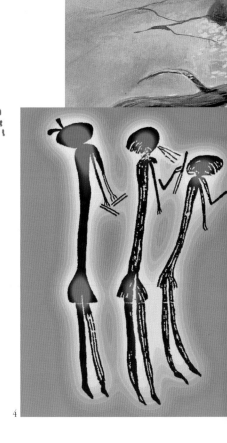

2. The left hemisphere of the human brain, showing the areas for articulate speech: at the left, Broca's Area, at the right, Wernicke's Area. Casts from inside the skull of Homo habilis *have shown a certain level of developmen of these areas, which leads us to believe that* Homo habilis *was capable of some form of speech. Furthermore, the transmission of skills for systematic stonecutting involves not just mimicking motions but also verbal instruction. There is a link between the use of the hand and verbal communication. The development of technology and the transmission of culture are chiefly a result of articulate speech dating from the oldest periods of human existence.*

3   4

5

3. *In prehistoric art, words are sometimes seen in tangible form, as if thoughts were materializing. This is one way of highlighting the primordial role of language. The arrow shows us three examples of this. In a rock painting in Tanzania, an individual is emitting a stream of word: lines are drawn coming out of his mouth (14000-8000 B.C.E.).*

4. *Again from Tanzania, a drawing of a rock painting in which three persons are perhaps intent on making music, but the person in the middle is making sounds orally (7000-3000 B.C.E.).*

5. *On the other side of the world, in Mexico, in the pre-Columbian city of Teotihuacán, we find the great mural from which this detail is taken: a man running, preceded by the comma shape, which, for the Mexican natives, was a symbol of speech (500 C.E.).*

DINNER

It has been a full day for Watu and the other men of the savanna. Now it is time for them to be with their families. It is the time for the communal meal, for sharing the food gathered during the day. The meat is divided up, along with rhizomes, herbs, and seeds. The long bones of the large animals (antelopes, zebras) are broken in half with choppers so that the marrow can be removed. Hollow gourds are used to carry water. And there is also fruit that the women have gathered and put aside.

During the meal, the people tell stories of the day's experiences. Watu recalls the large cats and the elephants that he came upon in the savanna and warns the young: "Never go off on your own, away from the camp. The savanna is not to be trusted because hungry predators may be hiding among the tall grasses . . . always be alert to snakes rustling in the grass, even though they usually run when people come close. And always be ready with sticks and stones."

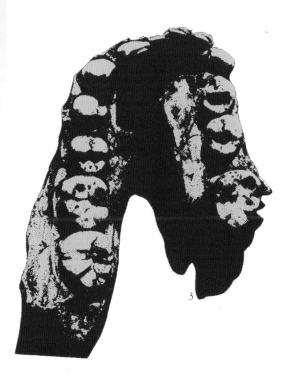

1. The vegetarian part of the diet of Homo habilis *was enriched by the earth's natural produce, which he sought and gathered.*

2. Finding a dead animal was an opportunity not to be missed by the first humans; they pooled their efforts to cut up the animal and transport it back to the camp, where it would later be eaten by the group.

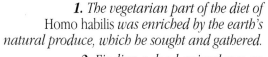

3. A mandible of Homo habilis *found at Olduvai (Tanzania). Optical and electronic microscopes have allowed scientists to make in-depth studies of the chewing surfaces of the teeth of* Homo habilis*. Many lines appear on the dental enamel. These would be the result of chewing, and they help reveal the type of diet of early humans and even the portion size of their omnivorous "menu."*

4. *A Tanzanian landscape at dusk.*

5. *At Olduvai,* Homo habilis *may have come across a wide variety of animals, some of which, now extinct, have been partially restored by bone fragments. These bones, which are sometimes found in the camps of the first humans, may be the remains of what was once a delicious dinner.*

5

THE EVENING: COUNCIL OF THE ELDERS

After the meal, while the children go outside the hut to play at being hunters and animals, the women tidy up the camp and the men get together. Each of them tells his impressions of the day, of the animals he has encountered, the dangers he has avoided.

Now Watu speaks: "This region can still offer resources. Later, we will settle in a place with new resources. Tomorrow, we should move in the direction opposite the sunrise, where there is water. We can follow the footprints of the antelopes and zebras. Maybe near the water we will find an animal to catch or some edible plants. In any case, we will need good equipment such as sticks and stones, and we must avoid going too far into the woods, where we might find ourselves in danger.

We can only trust the Australopithecines. They walk very much the way we do. They have a way of living that is different from ours. We show them respect and they do not bother us."

1. Night is falling on the savanna, which is dominated by the large baobab tree.

2. Stone circles that were arranged 1,800,000 years ago at an Olduvai camp. The setup of the living area tells us something about the cultural and psychological development of Homo habilis. It indicates typical human behavior. And since groups of primitive humans did not settle for long in one place, such organized activity, together with the regular, sequential steps for toolmaking (which is a complex task), could only have been carried out by a socialized group of people. This shows the great importance of group structure.

3. The importance of socialized groups influenced human history. The arrow points to a rock painting of the Bushmen (South Africa) dating from over 100 years ago; it shows a hut where the human figures are sitting so close together that they blend into one another.

4. From India, a family scene painted on rock: women and children with everyday objects about 5000 years ago.

5. Restored face of Australopithecus robustus, who lived together with Homo habilis. He practiced bipedalism, but being sturdy he moved around rather awkwardly.

41

SUNSET AND
THE CHANGING SKY

It is sunset, a blazing sunset. On the horizon, the sun has grown larger. It looks like a ball of fire that is igniting the savanna.

The little ones are going to sleep in the hut. Watu strolls around the camp. He exchanges a few words with some friends. It is already dark. A few voices can still be heard, then there is silence, which is broken by the call of some nocturnal animal or the rustling of some tall grass, moved by the wind.

Watu looks up and considers the heavens. The sky, dotted with stars, is set out in all its solemnity and splendor. The ever-changing sky seems to shift at night. In the silence of the savanna, Watu thinks about his day, about his life, an adventure that is not free from risk and in which he must think about what each new day will bring.

He ponders the meaning of his own existence, of the rhythms of nature all around him, of the thing that is bigger than himself, on which he seems to depend. Who rules the day and night, the movement of the stars, and the ever-changing sky?

1. A sunset.

2. A sky dense with stars. For Homo habilis, *the sky must have been a guide to the natural phenomena that had an impact on his survival. In human history, certain needs for physical order take on meanings that go beyond the basics; the creation of symbols will grow with the passage of time. This applies to the home, clothing, food, and also the sky.*

3. *The arrow shows us two extraordinary examples of how stars were destined to become a source of amazement and reflection. Everywhere and in various epochs, stars are a main feature of prehistoric rock art. From a decorated rock in Utah (U.S.): two human figures seem to be pondering the stars (950-1200 C.E.).*

4. *An example of rock art from the area around Salamanca (Spain) dating from about 5000 years ago: a man seems to be almost enveloped by celestial bodies that rotate above his head.*

GLOSSARY

Two ways in which Homo habilis *obtained food: He dug for rhizomes, and he gathered fruit.*

ARTICULATE SPEECH: Language produced by a combination of fairly simple sounds. These sounds are organized in such a way that the nervous system associates a meaning with the sounds and sound combinations.

AUSTRALOPITHECUS AND AUSTRALOPITHECINES: Primates that were related to humans, especially because they stood semi-erect. They lived from about 5–4 million to 1 million years ago, mostly in Africa. "*Australopithecus*" is the scientific name, "Australopithecines" is the English plural name.

The Australopithecines took refuge from predators by climbing trees.

BAOBAB: Enormous African tree (*Adansonia digitata*), known for the size of its trunk, which can reach a diameter of 33 feet (10 meters), and for its longevity, which can be as much as 400 years. It yields large flowers and an oval-shaped fruit whose pulp is edible.

BIPEDALISM: To walk on two legs. This is the way humans walk today. Many primates can occasionally walk on their lower limbs, but for humans, this is the only form of locomotion. Over time, bipedalism has resulted in the lengthening of the legs and an entire series of skeletal and muscular adjustments.

Some Australopithecines struggle with vultures and hyenas to ensure that they will get the animal carcass.

CEREBRALIZATION: The progressive increase in brain size, accompanied by more complex function.

CRANIAL CAPACITY: Volume of the braincase. It is measured in cubic centimeters.

ERECT POSTURE: Upright position of the body characterized by vertical alignment of the head with the spinal column and lower limbs. Such alignment is a necessary condition for bipedalism.

In the savanna, men armed with sticks fell an antelope.

FLAKE: Roughly short and wide tool obtained from a nucleus of stone by percussion.

FLINT: Sedimentary rock formed by the accumulation of various types of deposits. It was very useful in prehistoric tool making because of its fine grain and hardness.

FOSSIL: From the Latin word meaning "to dig." One actually needs to dig to find fossils, which are evidence of ancient living organisms preserved in layers of rock. Traces of prehistoric human activity, such as deposits of stones or bones, artifacts, imprints and footprints, all belong to the world of fossils.

A group of Homo habilis *in the shelter of a hut. Food is obtained by skinning a small mammal.*

FOSSILIZATION: A natural process of preservation made possible by the coming together of various favorable circumstances and phenomena linked to the nature of the organism and environmental conditions.

HAMMER: Stone tool, chosen for its shape and resistance, used to strike sharply a nucleus in order to detach a flake from it. (See also PERCUSSION).

LOCOMOTION: An animal's ability to move from one place to another. The movements can vary according to the animal's organs and environment (water, land, air).

MIOCENE: Geological period (23.5 to 5.3 million years ago) characterized by great climactic changes brought about by sharp movements of the Earth's crust.

NUCLEUS (or CORE): Block of stone from which many kinds of tools are made.

PERCUSSION: A strong blow with which a nucleus of stone is being hit to break off a flake. This can be done *directly* with a stone hammer, or *indirectly* by putting another stone between the nucleus and the hammer.

PERENNIAL GRASSES: Large family of plants that often grow large extensions at the ends, as those of the savanna do.

POD: Also called a *legume*, it is the fruit of leguminous plants. When it is ripe, it opens and its two parts reveal edible seeds of high nutritive value.

PRECISE GRIP: A gesture with which one can hold an object between the thumb and other fingers for small, delicate tasks.

PRIMATES: Group of live-bearing mammals that includes various species with increasing brain development. The story of their evolution begins about 60 million years ago.

REMAINS: From the Latin word meaning "found," these are objects discovered during systematic archeological investigations.

RHIZOME: Part of a plant stem that grows underground, similar to a root but sometimes bearing leaves or scales.

RIFT: The large split in the African continent that occurred during the Middle Miocene period, 17 million years ago. It brought about new environmental conditions that would play an important role in human evolution.

SITE: Place where remains of prehistoric humans and their activities have been found. Such remains, discovered by scientists during a series of archeological excavations, are then passed on to the next stage of research.

STRONG GRIP: A gesture with which one can seize an object firmly with the palm of the hand and the fingers.

Australopithecines eating roots and stems.

The first humans preferred to set up camp near water.

INDEX

PICTURE CREDITS

EDITORIALE JACA BOOK (Giorgio Bacchin): **15** (7), **16-17** (above); (Alessandro Bartolozzi): **8** (1,2), **12-13** (2), **20** (3); (Giovanna Belcastro): **32** (1 modified); (Remo Berselli): **29** (4); (Dulio Citi): **42** (1); (Annapaola Del Nevo): **34** (3); (Antonio Molino): **9** (6), **20** (1); (Michela Rangoni Machiavelli): **14** (4), **24** (2), **25** (4,5). EDITORIALE JACA BOOK/BOLOGNA UNIVERSITY MUSEUM OF ANTHROPOLOGY: **10** (1), **11** (4). CARLO MEAZZA: **42** (2). GIOVANNI PINNA: **29** (3), **34** (2).

Illustration sources faithfully reproduced or modified

Anati, Emmanuel. "The World's First Painters" in *The Human Adventure*. Jaca Book, Year 1, no.1, summer, 1986: **38** (4).

—— , edited by. *Art and Religion in Prehistory*, Valcamonica Symposium, 1979. Jaca Book/Edizioni del Centro, 1979: **43** (4).

—— *Origins of Art and Conceptuality*. Jaca Book, 1989: **36** (3).

—— *The Imaginary Museum of Prehistory: Rock Art of the World*. Jaca Book, 2002: **14** (2), **15** (5,6), **27** (3), **36** (4), **40** (1), **41** (4).

Broglio, Alberto, and Janusz Kozlowski. *Paleolithic Age*. Jaca Book, 1986: **11** (6, right).

Chavaillon, Jean. "Melka-Kunturé: Report on Discoveries" in *The Human Adventure*. Jaca Book, Year 2, no. 4, spring, 1987: **22** (1), **24** (1), **28** (1).

Coppens, Yves. "The Fossilized Human Brain," "Hominoids, Hominids and Humans," "The Evolution of Man," in *Proceedings of the Academy of Science*, 1981, 1984, 1986 [Italian translation, Jaca Book, 1996]: **8** (4), **41** (5).

—— "Horizons of Paleoanthropology," in *The Human Adventure*. Jaca Book, Year 1, no. 2, autumn, 1986: **20** (2), **26** (1), **38** (3).

—— *The Monkey, Africa and Mankind*. Arthème Fayard, 1983. [Italian translation, Jaca Book, 1996]: **10** (3), **11** (5), **24** (3).

De Lumley, Henry. *The Origin and Evolution of Man*. Laboratory of Prehistory of the Museum of Mankind and the National Museum of Natural History, Paris, 1983. [Italian translation, Jaca Book, 1985]: **40** (2).

Dué, Andrea, *From the Village to the City: Geography of the Neolithic Age*, vol. 2 of *The Atlas of the History of Mankind*. Jaca Book, 1993: **35** (4).

—— , edited by. *The First Inhabited Lands: From Primates to Homo Sapiens*, vol. 1 of *The Atlas of the History of Mankind*. Jaca Book, 1993: **12** (1), **39** (5), **44-45**.

Facchini, Fiorenzo. *The Path of Human Evolution*. Jaca Book, 1994: **36** (1).

—— *Origins: Man. Introduction to Paleoanthropology*. Jaca Book, 1990: **11** (6 left), **22** (2), **30** (1,2,3), **36** (2).

—— , edited by. *Paleoanthropology and Prehistory*, a volume of *The Open Thematic Encyclopedia*. Jaca Book, 1993: **16-17** (bottom), **31** (4).

Gimbutas, Marija. "Feminine Divinities in Neolithic Sardinia" in *The Human Adventure*. Jaca Book, Year 3, no. 8, spring, 1988: **32** (3).

Johanson, Donald C. "The Australopithecus: Current Problems," in *The Human Adventure*. Jaca Book, Year 4, no. 12, autumn, 1989: **9** (5), **10** (2).

Kozlowski, Janusz K. *Prehistory of Eastern European Art*. Jaca Book, 1992: **32** (2,4).

Lewis-Williams, James David. *Art of the Savanna: Rock Art Paintings of Southern Africa*. Jaca Book, 1983: **14** (3), **40** (3).

Matos Moctezuma Eduardo. *Teotihuacan*. Jaca Book, 1990: **37** (5).

Pinna, Giovanni. *Natural History of Europe: Six Hundred Million Years Through the Great Paleontological Sites*. Jaca Book, 1999: **34** (1).

Ries, Julien. *Origins: Religions*. Jaca Book, 1993: **43** (3).